Artisan Bread Recipes

Artisan Bread Cookbook Full of Easy, Simple And Mouthwatering Artisan Bread Recipes

By Marie Folher

Copyright Disclaimer

Disclaimer

Table of Contents

Introduction

Do you love baking? Or are you looking for a way to cut your grocery bill? You should start with bread because, for one, homemade bread costs half the amount you pay at a bakery. Secondly, it is healthier, tastier, and you know where your bread is coming from. And, nothing can replace the joy of devouring a warm slice of freshly-baked bread and filling your home with its inviting aroma, not even money. So, to begin your in-house baking journey, you should start with something real, chewy, crusty, and scrumptious loaves, something that completes your meal as well. And, one such loaf is artisan-style bread.

This 3000 years old bread is a new hype on the internet due to its freshness, wholesome ingredients, unique taste, and looks. With the carb contents in it, the flour and wheat used hand-crafted artisan bread along with other clean ingredients are actually good for you as it minimizes bloat due to being easier to digest.

Does it sound tough?! Traditional artisanal techniques are hard to get by. But trust me, you don't have to be a foodie or any pro baker to try your hand in artisan bread baking. With the rise in popularity, artisanal baking has embraced some modern conveniences. To be honest, there aren't any special restrictions to make it and how it is supposed to look like. You will get it when you eat it.

The only secret to success is picking quality ingredients and **patience**. Yes, it will take hours and sometimes, days, and even weeks to prepare this loaf, but it is all worth the wait. The loaf comes out beautiful, crusty, hearty, and delicious. And, once you realize how simple it is to bake a loaf of homemade artisan bread, you will find giving yourself an excuse to bake it often.

Now go bake some!

No-Knead Artisan Bread Recipes

Raisin Nut Bread

Preparation time: 12 hours and 45 minutes

Cooking time: 35 minutes

Total time: 13 hours and 20 minutes

Servings: 1 loaf, about 10 slices

Nutritional Info (Per Serving):

141 Cal | 1 g Fat | 1 g Protein | 30.6 g Carbs | 1.4 g Fiber

Ingredients:

13.75 ounces (3 cups + 2 tablespoons) / 390 grams **all-purpose flour**, and more as needed

0.05 ounces (½ teaspoon) / 1.5 grams **instant yeast**, dry

0.40 ounces (2 teaspoons) / 11 grams **sea salt**

3.5 ounces (1 cup) / 100 grams **raisins**

3.5 ounces (1 cup) / 100 grams chopped **pecans or walnuts**

0.75 ounces (1 tablespoon) / 21 grams **honey**

12 fluid ounces (1 ½ cups) / 355 grams (355 ml) **water**, at 100°F / 38°C

Directions:

1.   Prepare the dough and for this, take a large mixing bowl (preferably) with a resealable lid and then add all the ingredients in it except for water.

2.   Stir until mixed, then mix in water by using a wooden spoon or a stand mixer until incorporated and sticky mixture comes together.

3.   Cover the bowl with its lid (or plastic wrap / aluminum foil) and then let the dough rest at least for 12 hours at the room temperature until double in volume.

4.   Meanwhile, spread the parchment sheet on a clean working sheet and then sprinkle some flour on top of it.

5.   When the dough has risen, sprinkle some flour on the surface of the dough, pull up the dough, and place it onto the prepared parchment sheet.

6.   Shape the dough into a ball and for this, lift its edges towards the center by using lightly floured hands, tuck in the edges to make it round, turn the dough around seam side down, and then pat the sides to make the dough more round.

7.   Place the dough ball with the parchment into a large bowl or a proofing basket and then let it rest for 30 minutes.

8.   During the resting time, switch on the oven, place a large pot or a Dutch oven with its lid into it, then set it to 475°F / 245°C and let it preheat.

9.   After the 30 minutes, sprinkle some more flour onto the dough, make a ¼-inch / ½-cm deep X or slash on top of the dough by using a serrated knife, and then carefully place the dough into the pot with the parchment paper.

10. Cover the pot with the lid, bake the bread for 25 minutes, then uncover the pot and continue baking for 10 minutes until the crust of bread turns nicely brown.

11. When done, transfer the bread to a wire rack, cool it for 30 minutes, then cut it into slices and serve.

(Don't cut the bread until it has cooled completely. The bread continues to bake even after it has been removed from the oven. Cutting too early may result in the inside becoming rubbery)

Whole Wheat Bread

Preparation time: 19 hours and 15 minutes

Cooking time: 45 minutes

Total time: 20 hours

Servings: 1 loaf, about 10 slices

Nutritional Info (Per Serving):

130 Cal | 1 g Fat | 3 g Protein | 26 g Carbs | 1 g Fiber

Ingredients:

10 ounces (2 ¼ cups) /285 grams **all-purpose flour**, plus extra for dusting

0.05 ounces (½ teaspoon) / 1.5 grams **instant yeast**

5 ounces (1 1/5 cups) /140 grams **whole wheat flour**

1.5 ounces (2 tablespoons) / 42 grams **honey**

0.3 ounces (1 ½ teaspoons) / 8.5 grams **salt**

10 fluid ounces (1 ¼ cups) /280 grams (280 ml) **water**, at 100°F / 38°C

Directions:

1.   Prepare the dough and for this, take a large mixing bowl (preferably) with a resealable lid, add both flours, yeast, and salt in it and then stir until mixed.

2.   Take a separate large bowl, add honey in it and then whisk in water until combined.

3.   Pour honey mixture into the bowl containing flour and mix by using a wooden spoon or a stand mixer until incorporated and sticky mixture comes together.

4.   Cover the bowl with its lid (or plastic wrap / aluminum foil) and then let the dough rest for a minimum of 18 hours at the room temperature until double in volume.

5.   Meanwhile, spread the parchment sheet on a clean working sheet and then sprinkle some flour on top of it.

6.   When the dough has risen, sprinkle some flour on the surface of the dough, pull up the dough, and then place it onto the prepared parchment sheet.

7.   Shape the dough into a ball and for this, lift its edges towards the center by using lightly floured hands, tuck in the edges to make it round, turn the dough around seam side down, and then pat the sides to make the dough more round.

8.   Place the dough ball with the parchment into a large bowl or a proofing basket and let it rest for 45 minutes.

9.   During the resting time, switch on the oven, place a large pot or a Dutch oven with its lid into it, then set it to 400°F / 205°C and let it preheat.

10. After the 45 minutes, sprinkle some more flour onto the dough, make a ¼-inch / ½-cm deep X or slash on top of the dough by using a serrated knife, and then carefully place the dough into the pot with the parchment paper.

11. Cover the pot with the lid, bake the bread for 30 minutes, then uncover the pot and continue baking for 15 minutes until the crust of bread turns nicely brown.

12. When done, transfer the bread to a wire rack, cool it for 30 minutes, then cut it into slices and serve.

(Don't cut the bread until it has cooled completely. The bread continues to bake even after it has been removed from the oven. Cutting too early may result in the inside becoming rubbery)

Garlic and Rosemary Bread

Preparation time: 13 hours

Cooking time: 45 minutes

Total time: 13 hours and 45 minutes

Servings: 1 loaf, about 12 slices

Nutritional Info (Per Serving):

148 Cal | 0.8 g Fat | 3.5 g Protein | 27 g Carbs | 1 g Fiber

Ingredients:

13.2 ounces (3 cups) / 375 grams **all-purpose flour**

1 **head of garlic**

0.3 ounces (1 ½ teaspoons) / 8.5 grams **salt**

0.5 ounces (1 tablespoon) / 13 grams **olive oil**

0.05 ounces (½ teaspoon) / 1.5 grams **active yeast**, dry

12 fluid ounces (1 ½ cups) / 355 grams (355 ml) **water**, at 100°F / 38°C

1 tablespoon chopped **rosemary**, fresh

Directions:

1.   Roast the garlic and for this, switch on the oven, set it to 425°F / 220°C and let it preheat.

2.   Meanwhile, prepare the garlic, and for this, cut its top off the head so that cloves are exposed and then drizzle with the olive oil.

3.   Wrap garlic into a foil, roast for 45 minutes, and when done, cool for 15 minutes or more until garlic easily comes out of its skin.

4.   Prepare the dough and for this, take a large mixing bowl (preferably) with a resealable lid and then add garlic in it along with remaining ingredients except for water.

5.   Pour in water and then mix by using a wooden spoon or a stand mixer until incorporated and sticky mixture comes together.

6.   Cover the bowl with its lid (or plastic wrap / aluminum foil) and then let the dough rest for a minimum of 12 hours at the room temperature until double in volume.

7.   Meanwhile, spread the parchment sheet on a clean working sheet and then sprinkle some flour on top of it.

8.   When the dough has risen, sprinkle some flour on the surface of the dough, pull up the dough, and then place it onto the prepared parchment sheet.

9.   Shape the dough into a ball and for this, lift its edges towards the center by using lightly floured hands, tuck in the edges to make it round, turn the dough around seam side down, and then pat the sides to make the dough more round.

10.   Place the dough ball with the parchment into a large bowl or a proofing basket and let it rest for 30 minutes.

11. During the resting time, switch on the oven, place a large pot or a Dutch oven with its lid into it, then set it to 500°F / 260°C and let it preheat.

12. After the 30 minutes, sprinkle some flour on the surface of the dough, and then make a ¼-inch / ½-cm deep X or slash on top of the dough by using a serrated knife.

13. Carefully place the dough into the preheated pot with the parchment paper, cover the pot with the lid, bake the bread for 30 minutes, then uncover the pot and continue baking for 15 minutes until the crust of bread turns nicely brown.

14. When done, transfer the bread to a wire rack, cool it for 30 minutes, then cut it into slices and serve.

(Don't cut the bread until it has cooled completely. The bread continues to bake even after it has been removed from the oven. Cutting too early may result in the inside becoming rubbery)

Herb Crusted Artisan Bread

Preparation time: 13 hours and 45 minutes

Cooking time: 45 minutes

Total time: 14 hours and 30 minutes

Servings: 1 loaf, about 12 slices

Nutritional Info (Per Serving):

87.7 Cal | 1 g Fat | 2.8 g Protein | 16.6 g Carbs | 1 g Fiber

Ingredients:

13.2 ounces (3 cups) / 375 grams **all-purpose flour**

0.45 ounces (1 tablespoon) / 12.5 grams **sugar**

0.3 ounces (1 ½ teaspoons) / 8.5 grams **salt**

1 teaspoon dried **oregano**

0.16 ounces (1 ½ teaspoon) / 4.7 grams **instant yeast**, dry

½ teaspoon dried **rosemary**

½ teaspoon dried **basil**

0.7 ounces (1 ½ tablespoons) / 20 grams **olive oil**

12 fluid ounces (1 ½ cups) / 355 grams (355 ml) **water**, at 100°F / 38°C

2.6 ounces (3/4 cup) / 75 grams grated **parmesan cheese**

Directions:

1.   Prepare the dough and for this, take a large mixing bowl (preferably) with a resealable lid and then add flour, yeast, salt, and sugar in it, mix until combined.

2.   Add oil and all the herbs, pour in water, and then mix by using a wooden spoon or a stand mixer until incorporated and sticky mixture comes together.

3.   Cover the bowl with its lid (or plastic wrap / aluminum foil) and then let the dough rest for a minimum of 12 hours at the room temperature until double in volume.

4.   Meanwhile, spread the parchment sheet on a clean working sheet and then sprinkle some flour on top of it.

5.   When the dough has risen, sprinkle some flour on the surface of the dough, pull up the dough, and then place it onto the prepared parchment sheet.

6.   Stir in more flour until slightly dry and then add cheese and combine.

7.   Shape the dough into a ball and for this, lift its edges towards the center by using lightly floured hands, tuck in the edges to make it round, turn the dough around seam side down, and then pat the sides to make the dough more round.

8.   Sprinkle some more flour onto the dough, make a ¼-inch / ½-cm deep X or slash on top of the dough by using a serrated knife, and then carefully place it into a large pot with the parchment paper.

9.   Cover the pot with the lid, place it into an oven and let it rest for 1 hour and 30 minutes; don't switch on the oven.

10. Then remove the pot from the oven, switch on the oven, then set it to 425°F / 220°C and let it preheat.

11. Then return the pot into the oven, bake the bread for 30 minutes, then uncover the pot and continue baking for 15 minutes until the crust of bread turns nicely brown.

12. When done, transfer the bread to a wire rack, cool it for 30 minutes, then cut it into slices and serve.

(Don't cut the bread until it has cooled completely. The bread continues to bake even after it has been removed from the oven. Cutting too early may result in the inside becoming rubbery)

Multigrain Bread

Preparation time: 5 hours and 50 minutes

Cooking time: 45 minutes

Total time: 6 hours and 35 minutes

Servings: 1 loaf, about 12 slices

Nutritional Info (Per Serving):

69.1 Cal | 1.1 g Fat | 3.5 g Protein | 11.3 g Carbs | 2 g Fiber

Ingredients:

1.75 ounces (½ cup) / 50 grams **rye flour**

8.8 ounces (2 cups) / 250 grams **all-purpose flour**

0.4 ounces (2 tablespoons) / 11 grams **rolled oats**

2.1 ounces (½ cup) / 60 grams **whole-wheat flour**

0.8 ounces (2 tablespoons) / 22.5 grams **quinoa**

0.16 ounces (½ tablespoon) / 4.7 grams **active yeast**, dry

2 tablespoons **sunflower seeds**

0.45 ounces (¾ tablespoon) / 12.8 grams **salt**

1 fluid ounce (2 tablespoons) / 30 grams (30 ml) **water**, at room temperature

12 fluid ounces (1 ½ cups) / 355 grams (355 ml) **water**, at 100°F / 38°C

Directions:

1.   Take a small bowl, place quinoa, oats, and sunflower seeds in it, stir in 2 tablespoons of water and then let it rest for 1 hour.

2.   Then prepare the dough and for this, take a large mixing bowl (preferably) with a resealable lid and then add yeast and water in it.

3.   Mix by using a wooden spoon or a stand mixer until combined and then mix in all the flours, soaked oats mixture and salt until incorporated and sticky mixture comes together.

4.   Cover the bowl with its lid (or plastic wrap / aluminum foil) and then let the dough rest for a minimum of 4 hours at the room temperature until double in volume.

5.   Meanwhile, spread the parchment sheet on a clean working sheet and then sprinkle some flour on top of it.

6.   When the dough has risen, sprinkle some flour on the surface of the dough, pull up the dough, and then place it onto the prepared parchment sheet.

7.   Shape the dough into a ball and for this, lift its edges towards the center by using lightly floured hands, tuck in the edges to make it round, turn the dough around seam side down, and then pat the sides to make the dough more round.

8.   Place the dough ball with the parchment into a large bowl or a proofing basket and then let it rest for 40 minutes.

9.   During the resting time, switch on the oven, place a large pot or a Dutch oven with its lid into it, then set it to 450°F / 230°C and let it preheat.

10. After the 40 minutes, sprinkle some more flour onto the dough, make a ¼-inch / ½-cm deep X or slash on top of the dough by using a serrated knife, and then carefully place it into the pot with the parchment paper.

11. Cover the pot with the lid, bake the bread for 30 minutes, then uncover the pot and continue baking for 15 minutes until the crust of bread turns nicely brown.

12. When done, transfer the bread to a wire rack, cool it for 30 minutes, then cut it into slices and serve.

(Don't cut the bread until it has cooled completely. The bread continues to bake even after it has been removed from the oven. Cutting too early may result in the inside becoming rubbery)

Sourdough Bread

Preparation time: 14 hours and 50 minutes

Cooking time: 40 minutes

Total time: 15 hours and 30 minutes

Servings: 1 loaf, about 12 slices

Nutritional Info (Per Serving):

153 Cal | 1.5 g Fat | 1 g Protein | 33 g Carbs | 1.4 g Fiber

Ingredients:

9.2 ounces (2 cups) / 260 grams **whole wheat flour**

0.3 ounces (1 ½ teaspoons) / 8.5 grams **salt**

2.5 ounces (¼ cup) / 70 grams **sourdough starter**

9.2 ounces (2 cups) / 260 grams **white bread flour**, high-protein

14.85 fluid ounces (1 ¾ cups + 1 tablespoon) / 440 grams (440 ml) **water**, at 100°F / 38°C

Directions:

1.   Prepare the dough and for this, take a large mixing bowl (preferably) with a resealable lid, add the sourdough starter in it, and then pour in water.

2.   Add remaining ingredients and then mix by using a wooden spoon or a stand mixer until incorporated and sticky mixture comes together.

3.   Cover the bowl with its lid (or plastic wrap / aluminum foil) and then let the dough rest for a minimum of 12 hours at the room temperature until double in volume.

4.   Meanwhile, spread the parchment sheet on a clean working sheet and then sprinkle some flour on top of it.

5.   When the dough has risen, sprinkle some flour on the surface of the dough, pull up the dough, and then place it onto the prepared parchment sheet.

6.   Shape the dough into a ball and for this, lift its edges towards the center by using lightly floured hands, tuck in the edges to make it round, turn the dough around seam side down, and then pat the sides to make the dough more round.

7.   Place the dough ball with the parchment into a large bowl or a proofing basket and then let it rest for 90 minutes.

8.   During the resting time, switch on the oven, place a large pot or a Dutch oven with its lid into it, then set it to 500°F / 260°C and let it preheat.

9.   After the 90 minutes, sprinkle some more flour onto the dough, make a ¼-inch / ½-cm deep X or slash on top of the dough by using a serrated knife, and then carefully place it into the pot with the parchment paper.

10. Cover the pot with the lid, bake the bread for 17-20 minutes, then uncover the pot and continue baking for 15-20 minutes until the crust of bread turns nicely brown.

11. When done, transfer the bread to a wire rack, cool it for 30 minutes, then cut it into slices and serve.

(Don't cut the bread until it has cooled completely. The bread continues to bake even after it has been removed from the oven. Cutting too early may result in the inside becoming rubbery)

Cinnamon and Raisin Bread

Preparation time: 13 hours and 45 minutes

Cooking time: 45 minutes

Total time: 14 hours and 30 minutes

Servings: 1 loaf, about 12 slices

Nutritional Info (Per Serving):

90 Cal | 1.5 g Fat | 2 g Protein | 17 g Carbs | 0.5 g Fiber

Ingredients:

6.35 ounces (1 ½ cups) / 180 grams **all-purpose flour**

0.03 ounces (¼ teaspoon) / 0.8 grams **instant yeast**, dry

1 tablespoon **ground cinnamon**

6.35 ounces (1 ½ cups) / 180 grams **whole-wheat flour**

2.65 ounces (½ cup) / 75 grams **raisins**

0.3 ounces (1 ½ teaspoons) / 8.5 grams **salt**

2.65 ounces (½ cup) / 75 grams **walnuts**

12 fluid ounces (1 ½ cups) / 355 grams (355 ml) **water**, at 100°F / 38°C

Directions:

1.   Prepare the dough and for this, take a large mixing bowl (preferably) with a resealable lid and then add flours, salt, cinnamon, and yeast in it.

2.   Add raisins and nuts, pour in water, and then mix by using a wooden spoon or a stand mixer until incorporated and sticky mixture comes together.

3.   Cover the bowl with its lid (or plastic wrap / aluminum foil) and then let the dough rest for a minimum of 12 hours at the room temperature until double in volume.

4.   Meanwhile, take a separate large bowl, and then dust it with flour.

5.   When the dough has risen, sprinkle some flour on the surface of the dough, pull up this dough, and then shape the dough into a smooth ball.

6.   Place the dough ball into prepared bowl, cover with a plastic wrap, and then let it rest for 90 minutes.

7. During the resting time, switch on the oven, place a large pot or a Dutch oven with its lid into it, then set it to 500°F / 260°C and let it preheat.

8. After the 90 minutes, sprinkle some more flour onto the dough, make a ¼-inch / ½-cm deep X or slash on top of the dough by using a serrated knife, and then carefully place it into the pot with the parchment paper.

9. Cover the pot with the lid, bake the bread for 30 minutes, then uncover the pot and continue baking for 15 minutes until the crust of bread turns nicely brown.

10. When done, transfer the bread to a wire rack, cool it for 30 minutes, then cut it into slices and serve.

(Don't cut the bread until it has cooled completely. The bread continues to bake even after it has been removed from the oven. Cutting too early may result in the inside becoming rubbery)

Garlic and Sesame Seed Bread

Preparation time: 12 hours and 35 minutes

Cooking time: 45 minutes

Total time: 13 hours and 20 minutes

Servings: 1 loaf, about 12 slices

Nutritional Info (Per Serving):

106.1 Cal | 1.5 g Fat | 1.3 g Protein | 20.3 g Carbs | 1.7 g Fiber

Ingredients:

12.7 ounces (3 cups) / 360 grams **whole-wheat flour**

0.05 ounces (½ teaspoon) / 1.5 grams **active yeast, dry**

1 teaspoon **mixed dried herbs**

2 teaspoons **chopped garlic**

0.18 ounces (1 teaspoon) / 5.2 grams **sugar**

½ teaspoon dried **rosemary**

0.2 ounces (1 teaspoon) / 5.7 grams **salt**

0.65 ounces (1 tablespoon + 1 teaspoon) / 18 grams **olive oil**

12 fluid ounces (1 ½ cups) / 355 grams (355 ml) **water**, at 100°F / 38°C

2 fluid ounces (¼ cup) / 60 grams (60 ml) **water**, at room temperature

1 teaspoon **sesame seeds**

Directions:

1.   Take a small bowl, add sugar and yeast in it, pour in 2 fl oz / 60 ml water, stir until sugar has dissolved, then cover the bowl and let it rest for 15 minutes.

2.   Then prepare the dough and for this, take a large mixing bowl (preferably) with a resealable lid and then add flour in it.

3.   Add salt and yeast mixture, pour in the remaining water, mix by using a wooden spoon or a stand mixer until incorporated, add oil and then continue mixing until sticky mixture comes together.

4.   Cover the bowl with its lid (or plastic wrap / aluminum foil) and then let the dough rest for a minimum of 12 hours at the room temperature until double in volume.

5.   When the resting time of the dough is about to end, switch on the oven, place a large pot or a Dutch oven with its lid into it, then set it to 475°F / 250°C and let it preheat.

6.   Meanwhile, spread the parchment sheet on a clean working sheet and then sprinkle some flour on top of it.

7.   When the dough has risen, add garlic, all the herbs, and spices into the dough and mix until just combined.

8.   Sprinkle some flour on the surface of the dough, pull up the dough, and then place it onto the prepared parchment sheet.

9.   Shape the dough into a ball and for this, lift its edges towards the center by using lightly floured hands, tuck in the edges to make it round, turn the dough around seam side down, and then pat the sides to make the dough more round.

10. Sprinkle some more flour onto the dough, make a ¼-inch / ½-cm deep X or slash on top of the dough by using a serrated knife, and then sprinkle sesame seeds on the surface of the dough.

11. Carefully place the dough into the preheated pot with the parchment paper, cover the pot with the lid, bake the bread for 30 minutes, then uncover the pot and continue baking for 15 minutes until the crust of bread turns nicely brown.

12. When done, transfer the bread to a wire rack, cool it for 30 minutes, then cut it into slices and serve.

(Don't cut the bread until it has cooled completely. The bread continues to bake even after it has been removed from the oven. Cutting too early may result in the inside becoming rubbery)

Cranberries and Walnut Bread

Preparation time: 15 hours and 15 minutes

Cooking time: 45 minutes

Total time: 16 hours

Servings: 1 loaf, about 12 slices

Nutritional Info (Per Serving):

114 Cal | 3 g Fat | 2 g Protein | 18 g Carbs | 3 g Fiber

Ingredients:

13.4 ounces (3 cups) / 380 grams **bread flour**

0.9 ounces (3 tablespoons) / 25 grams chopped dried **cranberries**

0.40 ounces (2 teaspoons) / 11 grams **salt**

¼ teaspoon ground **cumin**

0.5 ounces (4 tablespoons) / 13.5 grams chopped **sun-dried tomatoes**

½ teaspoon ground **coriander**

0.03 ounces (¼ teaspoon) / 0.8 grams **instant yeast**, dry

¼ teaspoon ground **fennel**

1.15 ounces (4 tablespoons) / 32.5 grams **hazelnuts**

0.75 ounces (1 tablespoon) / 21 grams **honey**

10.65 fluid ounces (1 1/3 cups) / 315 ml **water**, at 65°F / 18°C

Directions:

1.   Prepare the dough and for this, take a large mixing bowl (preferably) with a resealable lid and then add all the ingredients except for water.

2.   Stir until just mixed, pour in water, and then mix by using a wooden spoon or a stand mixer until incorporated and sticky mixture comes together.

3.   Cover the bowl with its lid (or plastic wrap / aluminum foil) and then let the dough rest for at least 14 hours at the room temperature until double in volume.

4.   Meanwhile, spread the parchment sheet on a clean working sheet and then sprinkle some flour on top of it.

5.   When the dough has risen, sprinkle some flour on the surface of the dough, pull up the dough, and then place it onto the prepared parchment sheet.

6.   Shape the dough into a ball and for this, lift its edges towards the center by using lightly floured hands, tuck in the edges to make it round, turn the dough around seam side down, and then pat the sides to make the dough more round.

7.   Place the dough ball with the parchment into a large bowl or a proofing basket and then let it rest for 60 minutes.

8.   During the resting time, switch on the oven, place a large pot or a Dutch oven with its lid into it, then set it to 475°F / 250°C and let it preheat.

9.   After the 60 minutes, sprinkle some more flour onto the dough, make a ¼-inch / ½-cm deep X or slash on top of the dough by using a serrated knife, and then carefully place it into the pot with the parchment paper.

10. Cover the pot with the lid, bake the bread for 30 minutes, then uncover the pot and continue baking for 15 minutes until the crust of bread turns nicely brown.

11. When done, transfer the bread to a wire rack, cool it for 30 minutes, then cut it into slices and serve.

(Don't cut the bread until it has cooled completely. The bread continues to bake even after it has been removed from the oven. Cutting too early may result in the inside becoming rubbery)

Blueberry and Walnut Bread

Preparation time: 12 hours and 45 minutes

Cooking time: 50 minutes

Total time: 13 hours and 35 minutes

Servings: 1 loaf, about 12 slices

Nutritional Info (Per Serving):

164 Cal | 2.8 g Fat | 9.4 g Protein | 24.6 g Carbs | 4.6 g Fiber

Ingredients:

1.4 ounces (¼ cup) / 40 grams dried **blueberries**

13.2 ounces (3 cups) / 375 grams **all-purpose flour**

0.40 ounces (2 teaspoons) / 11 grams **salt**

0.07 ounces (½ teaspoon) / 2 grams **active yeast**, dry

1.4 ounces (4 tablespoons) / 40 grams chopped **walnut**

12 fluid ounces (1 ½ cups) / 355 grams (355 ml) **water**, at 100°F / 38°C

Directions:

1.   Prepare the dough and for this, take a large mixing bowl (preferably) with a resealable lid and then add all the ingredients except for water.

2.   Stir until just mixed, pour in water, and then mix by using a wooden spoon or a stand mixer until incorporated and sticky mixture comes together.

3.   Cover the bowl with its lid (or plastic wrap / aluminum foil) and then let the dough rest for a minimum of 12 hours at the room temperature until double in volume.

4.   Meanwhile, spread the parchment sheet on a clean working sheet and then sprinkle some flour on top of it.

5.   When the dough has risen, sprinkle some flour on the surface of the dough, pull up the dough, and then place it onto the prepared parchment sheet.

6.   Shape the dough into a ball and for this, lift its edges towards the center by using lightly floured hands, tuck in the edges to make it round, turn the dough around seam side down, and then pat the sides to make the dough more round.

7.   Place the dough ball with the parchment into a large bowl or a proofing basket and then let it rest for 30 minutes.

8.   During the resting time, switch on the oven, place a large pot or a Dutch oven with its lid into it, then set it to 450°F / 230°C and let it preheat.

9.   After 30 minutes, sprinkle some more flour onto the dough, make a ¼-inch / ½-cm deep X or slash on top of the dough by using a serrated knife, and then carefully place it into the pot with the parchment paper.

10.   Cover the pot with the lid, bake the bread for 35 minutes, then uncover the pot and continue baking for 15 minutes until the crust of bread turns nicely brown.

11.   When done, transfer the bread to a wire rack, cool it for 30 minutes, then cut it into slices and serve.

(Don't cut the bread until it has cooled completely. The bread continues to bake even after it has been removed from the oven. Cutting too early may result in the inside becoming rubbery)

Cinnamon, Raisin and Pecan Bread

Preparation time: 12 hours and 45 minutes

Cooking time: 45 minutes

Total time: 13 hours and 30 minutes

Servings: 1 loaf, about 12 slices

Nutritional Info (Per Serving):

140 Cal | 4 g Fat | 1.6 g Protein | 23 g Carbs | 1 g Fiber

Ingredients:

14.3 ounces (3 ¼ cups) / 405 grams cup **all-purpose flour**

2.65 ounces (½ cup) / 75 grams **raisins**, fresh

0.35 ounces (1 ¾ teaspoons) / 10 grams **sea salt**

0.05 ounces (½ teaspoon) / 1.5 grams **active yeast**, dry

2.65 ounces (½ cup) / 75 grams chopped **toasted pecans**

1 ¾ teaspoon ground **cinnamon**

13.2 fluid ounces (1.65 cups) / 390 grams (390 ml) **water**, at 100°F / 38°C

Directions:

1.   Prepare the dough and for this, take a large mixing bowl (preferably) with a resealable lid and then add flour in it along with salt, yeast, and cinnamon.

2.   Stir until mixed, pour in water, and then mix by using a wooden spoon or a stand mixer until incorporated and sticky mixture comes together. Add raisins and pecans and mix until combined.

3.   Cover the bowl with its lid (or plastic wrap / aluminum foil) and then let the dough rest for a minimum of 12 hours at the room temperature until double in volume.

4.   Meanwhile, spread the parchment sheet on a clean working sheet and then sprinkle some flour on top of it.

5.   When the dough has risen, sprinkle some flour on the surface of the dough, pull up the dough, and then place it onto the prepared parchment sheet.

6. Shape the dough into a ball and for this, lift its edges towards the center by using lightly floured hands, tuck in the edges to make it round, turn the dough around seam side down, and then pat the sides to make the dough more round.

7. Place the dough ball with the parchment into a large bowl or a proofing basket and then let it rest for 30 minutes.

8. During the resting time, switch on the oven, place a large pot or a Dutch oven with its lid into it, then set it to 450°F / 230°C and let it preheat.

9. After the 30 minutes, sprinkle some more flour onto the dough, make a ¼-inch / ½-cm deep X or slash on top of the dough by using a serrated knife, and then carefully place it into the pot with the parchment paper.

10. Cover the pot with the lid, bake the bread for 30 minutes, then uncover the pot and continue baking for 12-15 minutes until the crust of bread turns nicely brown.

11. When done, transfer the bread to a wire rack, cool it for 30 minutes, then cut it into slices and serve.

(Don't cut the bread until it has cooled completely. The bread continues to bake even after it has been removed from the oven. Cutting too early may result in the inside becoming rubbery)

Jalapeno Cheese Bread

Preparation time: 13 hours

Cooking time: 45 minutes

Total time: 13 hours and 45 minutes

Servings: 1 loaf, about 12 slices

Nutritional Info (Per Serving):

181Cal | 5.2 g Fat | 7.1 g Protein | 25 g Carbs | 1 g Fiber

Ingredients:

13.2 ounces (3 cups) / 375 grams **all-purpose flour**

0.05 ounces (½ teaspoon) / 1.5 grams **instant yeast**, dry

0.40 ounces (2 teaspoons) / 11 grams **sea salt**

5.3 ounces (1 ½ cups) / 150 grams grated **cheddar cheese**

1.6 ounces (½ cup) / 45 grams sliced **jalapenos**, pickled

12 fluid ounces / 355 grams (355 ml) **water**, at room temperature

Directions:

1.   Prepare the dough and for this, take a large mixing bowl (preferably) with a resealable lid and then add flour in it along with yeast and salt, stir until mixed.

2.   Add cheese and jalapenos, stir until well coated, pour in water and then mix by using a wooden spoon or a stand mixer until incorporated and sticky mixture comes together.

3.   Cover the bowl with its lid (or plastic wrap / aluminum foil) and then let the dough rest for a minimum of 12 hours at the room temperature until double in volume.

4.   Meanwhile, spread the parchment sheet on a clean working sheet and then sprinkle some flour on top of it.

5.   When the dough has risen, sprinkle some flour on the surface of the dough, pull up the dough, and then place it onto the prepared parchment sheet.

6.   Shape the dough into a ball and for this, lift its edges towards the center by using lightly floured hands, tuck in the edges to make it round, turn the dough around seam side down, and then pat the sides to make the dough more round.

7.   Place the dough ball with the parchment into a large bowl or a proofing basket and then let it rest for 45 minutes.

8.   During the resting time, switch on the oven, place a large pot or a Dutch oven with its lid into it, then set it to 450°F / 230°C and let it preheat.

9.   After the 45 minutes, sprinkle some more flour onto the dough, make a ¼-inch / ½-cm deep X or slash on top of the dough by using a serrated knife, and then carefully place it into the pot with the parchment paper.

10. Cover the pot with the lid, bake the bread for 30 minutes, then uncover the pot and continue baking for 15 minutes until the crust of bread turns nicely brown.

11. When done, transfer the bread to a wire rack, cool it for 30 minutes, then cut it into slices and serve.

(Don't cut the bread until it has cooled completely. The bread continues to bake even after it has been removed from the oven. Cutting too early may result in the inside becoming rubbery)

Italian Bread

Preparation time: 12 hours and 45 minutes

Cooking time: 40 minutes

Total time: 13 hours and 25 minutes

Servings: 1 loaf, about 16 slices

Nutritional Info (Per Serving):

94 Cal | 1 g Fat | 2.3 g Protein | 20 g Carbs | 1.5 g Fiber

Ingredients:

13.2 ounces (3 cups) / 375 grams **all-purpose flour**

5 cloves of **garlic**, peeled, smashed

0.40 ounces (2 teaspoons) / 11 grams **salt**

2 tablespoons **Italian seasoning**

0.05 ounces (½ teaspoon) / 1.5 grams **instant yeast, dry**

12 fluid ounces / 355 grams (355 ml) **water**, at 80°F / 25°C

Directions:

1.   Prepare the dough and for this, take a large mixing bowl (preferably) with a resealable lid and then add flour in it along with salt and yeast, stir until mixed.

2.   Pour in water, and then mix by using a wooden spoon or a stand mixer until incorporated and sticky mixture comes together.

3.   Cover the bowl with its lid (or plastic wrap / aluminum foil) and then let the dough rest for a minimum of 12 hours at the room temperature until double in volume.

4.   Meanwhile, spread the parchment sheet on a clean working sheet and then sprinkle some flour on top of it.

5.   When the dough has risen, sprinkle some flour on the surface of the dough, pull up the dough, and then place it onto the prepared parchment sheet.

6.   Shape the dough into a ball and for this, lift its edges towards the center by using lightly floured hands, tuck in the edges to make it round, turn the dough around seam side down, and then pat the sides to make the dough more round.

7. Sprinkle Italian seasoning onto the surface of the dough and then spread smashed garlic evenly on it.

8. Place the dough ball with the parchment into a large bowl or a proofing basket and then let it rest for 30 minutes.

9. During the resting time, switch on the oven, place a large pot or a Dutch oven with its lid into it, then set it to 450°F / 230°C and let it preheat.

10. After 30 minutes, sprinkle some more flour onto the dough, make a ¼-inch / ½-cm deep X or slash on top of the dough by using a serrated knife, and then carefully place it into the pot with the parchment paper.

11. Cover the pot with the lid, bake the bread for 30 minutes, then uncover the pot and continue baking for 10 minutes until the crust of bread turns nicely brown.

12. When done, transfer the bread to a wire rack, cool it for 30 minutes, then cut it into slices and serve.

(Don't cut the bread until it has cooled completely. The bread continues to bake even after it has been removed from the oven. Cutting too early may result in the inside becoming rubbery)

Basil and Onion Bread

Preparation time: 13 hours and 10 minutes

Cooking time: 45 minutes

Total time: 13 hours and 55 minutes

Servings: 1 loaf, about 12 slices

Nutritional Info (Per Serving):

130 Cal | 1.6 g Fat | 1.1 g Protein | 24.8 g Carbs | 1.2 g Fiber

Ingredients:

10.05 ounces (2 ¼ cups) / 285 grams **bread flour**

0.28 ounces (2 teaspoons) / 8 grams **sugar**, divided

4.25 ounces (1 cup) / 120 grams **whole-wheat flour**

2.65 ounces (½ cup) / 75 grams sliced **white onion**

0.6 ounces (1 tablespoon) / 17 grams **salt**

0.11 ounces (1 teaspoon) / 3 grams **active yeast**, dry

0.35 ounces (½ cup) / 10 grams sliced **basil**

12 fluid ounces (1 ½ cups) / 355 grams (355 ml) **water**, at 110°F / 43°C

Directions:

1.   Take a small bowl, pour in water, add yeast, stir in half of the sugar (1 teaspoon) until it has dissolved, and then let it rest for 10 minutes.

2.   Prepare the dough and for this, take a large mixing bowl (preferably) with a resealable lid and then add the flours in it along with salt and remaining sugar.

3.   Stir until mixed, pour in yeast mixture, and then mix by using a wooden spoon or a stand mixer until incorporated and sticky mixture comes together.

4.   Cover the bowl with its lid (or plastic wrap / aluminum foil) and then let the dough rest for a minimum of 12 hours at the room temperature until double in volume.

5.   Meanwhile, spread the parchment sheet on a clean working sheet and then sprinkle some flour on top of it.

6. When the dough has risen, sprinkle some flour on the surface of the dough, pull up the dough, and then place it onto the prepared parchment sheet.

7. Shape the dough into a rectangle, evenly spread onion and basil on top, fold one-third of the dough in, fold over the other half, and keep repeating until a dough ball comes together.

8. Place the dough ball with the parchment into a large bowl or a proofing basket and then let it rest for 45 minutes at a warm place.

9. During the resting time, switch on the oven, place a large pot or a Dutch oven with its lid into it, then set it to 450°F / 230°C and let it preheat.

10. After the 45 minutes, sprinkle some more flour onto the dough, make a ¼-inch / ½-cm deep X or slash on top of the dough by using a serrated knife, and then carefully place it into the pot with the parchment paper.

11. Cover the pot with the lid, bake the bread for 30 minutes, then uncover the pot and continue baking for 15 minutes until the crust of bread turns nicely brown.

12. When done, transfer the bread to a wire rack, cool it for 30 minutes, then cut it into slices and serve.

(Don't cut the bread until it has cooled completely. The bread continues to bake even after it has been removed from the oven. Cutting too early may result in the inside becoming rubbery)

Rosemary and Lemon Bread

Preparation time: 14 hours and 15 minutes

Cooking time: 45 minutes

Total time: 15 hours

Servings: 1 loaf, about 12 slices

Nutritional Info (Per Serving):

118 Cal | 3.4 g Fat | 1.3 g Protein | 19 g Carbs | 0.8 g Fiber

Ingredients:

13.2 ounces (3 cups) / 375 grams **all-purpose flour**

0.35 ounces (1 ¾ teaspoons) / 10 grams **sea salt**

0.03 ounces (¼ teaspoon) / 0.8 grams **instant yeast**, dry

2 teaspoons **lemon zest**

2 teaspoons chopped **rosemary**, fresh

13.2 fluid ounces (1 ½ cups + 2 tablespoons) / 390 grams (390 ml) **water**, at 80°F / 25°C

Directions:

1.   Prepare the dough and for this, take a large mixing bowl (preferably) with a resealable lid and then add flour in it along with salt, yeast, lemon zest, and rosemary.

2.   Stir until mixed, pour in water, and then mix by using a wooden spoon or a stand mixer until incorporated and sticky mixture comes together.

3.   Cover the bowl with its lid (or plastic wrap / aluminum foil) and then let the dough rest for a minimum of 12 hours at the room temperature until double in volume.

4.   Meanwhile, spread the parchment sheet on a clean working sheet and then sprinkle some flour on top of it.

5.   When the dough has risen, sprinkle some flour on the surface of the dough, pull up the dough, and then place it onto the prepared parchment sheet.

6.   Shape the dough into a ball and for this, lift its edges towards the center by using lightly floured hands, tuck in the edges to make it round, turn the dough around seam side down, and then pat the sides to make the dough more round.

7.   Place the dough ball with the parchment into a large bowl or a proofing basket and then let it rest for 2 hours.

8.   During the resting time, switch on the oven, place a large pot or a Dutch oven with its lid into it, then set it to 450°F / 230°C and let it preheat.

9.   After the 2 hours, sprinkle some more flour onto the dough, make a ¼-inch / ½-cm deep X or slash on top of the dough by using a serrated knife, and then carefully place it into the pot with the parchment paper.

10. Cover the pot with the lid, bake the bread for 30 minutes, then uncover the pot and continue baking for 15 minutes until the crust of bread turns nicely brown.

11. When done, transfer the bread to a wire rack, cool it for 30 minutes, then cut it into slices and serve.

(Don't cut the bread until it has cooled completely. The bread continues to bake even after it has been removed from the oven. Cutting too early may result in the inside becoming rubbery)

Olive Bread

Preparation time: 13 hours and 15 minutes

Cooking time: 45 minutes

Total time: 14 hours

Servings: 1 loaf, about 10 slices

Nutritional Info (Per Serving):

162 Cal | 2.7 g Fat | 4.6 g Protein | 28.3 g Carbs | 1 g Fiber

Ingredients:

12.15 ounces (2 ¾ cups) / 345 grams **all-purpose flour**

3.2 ounces (½ cup) / 90 grams chopped **Kalamata olives**, pitted

½ teaspoon **garlic powder**

0.1 ounces (½ teaspoon) / 2.8 grams **salt**

0.16 ounces (1 ½ teaspoons) / 4.7 grams **active yeast**, dry

0.3 ounces (2 teaspoons) / 8.9 grams **olive oil**

8 fluid ounces / 240 grams (240 ml) **water**, at 80°F / 25°C

Directions:

1.   Prepare the dough and for this, take a large mixing bowl (preferably) with a resealable lid, add all the ingredients in it except for olives, stir until just combined, and then let it rest for 15 minutes.

2.   Then fold in olives and mix by using a wooden spoon or a stand mixer until incorporated and sticky mixture comes together.

3.   Cover the bowl with its lid (or plastic wrap / aluminum foil) and then let the dough rest for at least 12 hours at a warm place until double in volume.

4.   Meanwhile, spread the parchment sheet on a clean working sheet and then sprinkle some flour on top of it.

5.   When the dough has risen, sprinkle some flour on the surface of the dough, pull up the dough, and then place it onto the prepared parchment sheet.

6.   Shape the dough into a ball and for this, lift its edges towards the center by using lightly floured hands, tuck in the edges to make it round, turn the dough around seam side down, and then pat the sides to make the dough more round.

7.   Place the dough ball with the parchment into a large bowl or a proofing basket and then let it rest for 45 minutes at a warm place.

8.   During the resting time, switch on the oven, place a large pot or a Dutch oven with its lid into it, then set it to 400°F / 200°C and let it preheat.

9.   After the 45 minutes, sprinkle some more flour onto the dough, make a ¼-inch / ½-cm deep X or slash on top of the dough by using a serrated knife, and then carefully place it into the pot with the parchment paper.

10. Cover the pot with the lid, bake the bread for 30 minutes, then uncover the pot and continue baking for 15 minutes until the crust of bread turns nicely brown.

11. When done, transfer the bread to a wire rack, cool it for 30 minutes, then cut it into slices and serve.

(Don't cut the bread until it has cooled completely. The bread continues to bake even after it has been removed from the oven. Cutting too early may result in the inside becoming rubbery)

Graham Bread

Preparation time: 15 minutes

Cooking time: 45 minutes

Total time: 1 hour

Servings: 2 loaves, about 16 slices

Nutritional Info (Per Serving):

195 Cal | 2.3 g Fat | 4.7 g Protein | 39 g Carbs | 2.2 g Fiber

Ingredients:

12.7 ounces (3 cups) / 360 grams **whole-wheat graham flour**

8.8 ounces (1 cup) / 250 grams of **sugar**

0.53 ounces (2 ½ teaspoons) / 15 grams **baking soda**

4.25 ounces (1 cup) / 120 grams **whole-wheat flour**

0.1 ounces (½ teaspoon) / 2.8 grams **salt**

1 **egg**, at room temperature

21.15 fluid ounces (2 ½ cups) / 600 grams (585 ml) **buttermilk**

Directions:

1.   Switch on the oven, then set it to 350°F / 175°C and let it preheat.

2.   Meanwhile, take a large bowl, place flour in it, and then whisk in salt and baking soda until well combined.

3.   Take a separate large bowl, crack the egg in it and then beat in sugar until combined.

4.   Beat in flour mixture and milk alternately until incorporated and then divide the mixture evenly between two greased loaf pans.

5.   Bake the loaves for 45 minutes until the top has turned golden brown and set.

6.   Let bread cool in the pan for 15 minutes and then transfer them to a wire rack to cool completely.

7.   Slice each bread into eight pieces and then serve.

Whole-Wheat Walnut Bread

Preparation time: 18 hours and 55 minutes

Cooking time: 45 minutes

Total time: 19 hours and 40 minutes

Servings: 1 loaf, about 12 slices

Nutritional Info (Per Serving):

172 Cal | 8.5 g Fat | 5.2 g Protein | 21.2 g Carbs | 4 g Fiber

Ingredients:

16.9 ounces (4 cups) / 480 grams **whole-wheat flour**

0.11 ounces (1 teaspoon) / 3 grams **active yeast**, dry

0.45 ounces (1 tablespoon) / 12.5 grams **sugar**

6.7 ounces (1 ½ cups) / 190 grams **chopped walnuts**

0.2 ounces (1 teaspoon) / 5.7 grams **salt**

18.25 fluid ounces (2 ¼ cups) / 540 grams (540 ml) **water**, at 80°F / 25°C

Directions:

1.   Take a large mixing bowl (preferably) with a resealable lid, pour in water, add yeast and half of the flour, stir in sugar until it has dissolved, and let it rest for 1 minute.

2.   Cover the bowl with its lid (or plastic wrap / aluminum foil) and then let the dough rest for a minimum of 12 hours at the room temperature until double in volume.

3.   Then add remaining flour and salt, mix by using a wooden spoon or a stand mixer until incorporated and sticky mixture comes together and then fold in nuts until well combined.

4.   Return cover on the bowl and then let the dough rest for at least 6 hours at the room temperature until double in volume.

5.   Meanwhile, spread the parchment sheet on a clean working sheet and then sprinkle some flour on top of it.

6.   When the dough has risen, sprinkle some flour on the surface of the dough, pull up the dough, and then place it onto the prepared parchment sheet.

7.   Shape the dough into a ball and for this, lift its edges towards the center by using lightly floured hands, tuck in the edges to make it round, turn the dough around seam side down, and then pat the sides to make the dough more round.

8.   Place the dough ball with the parchment into a large bowl or a proofing basket and then let it rest for 90 minutes at a warm place.

9.   During the resting time, switch on the oven, place a large pot or a Dutch oven with its lid into it, then set it to 375°F / 190°C and let it preheat.

10.   After the 90 minutes, sprinkle some more flour onto the dough, make a ¼-inch / ½-cm deep X or slash on top of the dough by using a serrated knife, and then carefully place it into the pot with the parchment paper.

11. Cover the pot with the lid, bake the bread for 30 minutes, then uncover the pot and continue baking for 15 minutes until the crust of bread turns nicely brown.

12. When done, transfer the bread to a wire rack, cool it for 30 minutes, then cut it into slices and serve.

(Don't cut the bread until it has cooled completely. The bread continues to bake even after it has been removed from the oven. Cutting too early may result in the inside becoming rubbery)

Lemon and Thyme Bread

Preparation time: 19 hours

Cooking time: 45 minutes

Total time: 19 hours and 45 minutes

Servings: 1 loaf, about 10 slices

Nutritional Info (Per Serving):

161 Cal | 1 g Fat | 5 g Protein | 31 g Carbs | 1.5 g Fiber

Ingredients:

13.2 ounces (3 cups) / 375 grams **all-purpose flour**

0.11 ounces (1 teaspoon) / 3 grams **wheat gluten**

0.50 ounces (3 teaspoons) / 14.4 grams **baking powder**

0.22 ounces (2 teaspoons) / 6.2 grams **active yeast**, dry

2 teaspoons **lemon zest**

2 teaspoons **Mrs. Dash Table Blend**

1 teaspoon dried **thyme**

12 fluid ounces (1 ½ cups) / 355 grams (355 ml) **water**, at 80°F / 25°C

Directions:

1.   Prepare the dough and for this, take a large mixing bowl (preferably) with a resealable lid and then add all the ingredients in it except for water.

2.   Stir until mixed, pour in water, and then mix by using a wooden spoon or a stand mixer until incorporated and sticky mixture comes together.

3.   Cover the bowl with its lid (or plastic wrap / aluminum foil) and then let the dough rest for a minimum of 18 hours at the room temperature until double in volume.

4.   Meanwhile, spread the parchment sheet on a clean working sheet and then sprinkle some flour on top of it.

5.   When the dough has risen, sprinkle some flour on the surface of the dough, pull up the dough, and then place it onto the prepared parchment sheet.

6.   Shape the dough into a ball and for this, lift its edges towards the center by using lightly floured hands, tuck in the edges to make it round, turn the dough around seam side down, and then pat the sides to make the dough more round.

7.   Place the dough ball with the parchment into a large bowl or a proofing basket and then let it rest for 45 minutes at a warm place.

8.   During the resting time, switch on the oven, place a large pot or a Dutch oven with its lid into it, then set it to 450°F / 230°C and let it preheat.

9.   After the 45 minutes, sprinkle some more flour onto the dough, make a ¼-inch / ½-cm deep X or slash on top of the dough by using a serrated knife, and then carefully place it into the pot with the parchment paper.

10.   Cover the pot with the lid, bake the bread for 30 minutes, then uncover the pot and continue baking for 15 minutes until the crust of bread turns nicely brown.

11. When done, transfer the bread to a wire rack, cool it for 30 minutes, then cut it into slices and serve.

(Don't cut the bread until it has cooled completely. The bread continues to bake even after it has been removed from the oven. Cutting too early may result in the inside becoming rubbery)

Pumpkin Spice Bread

Preparation time: 1 hour and 20 minutes

Cooking time: 50 minutes

Total time: 2 hours and 10 minutes

Servings: 1 loaf, about 12 slices

Nutritional Info (Per Serving):

178 Cal | 7 g Fat | 2.1 g Protein | 28 g Carbs | 1 g Fiber

Ingredients:

16 ounces (3 ½ cups + 2 tablespoons) / 455 grams **all-purpose flour**

0.45 ounces (1 tablespoon) / 12.5 grams **sugar**

1 tablespoon **garam masala**

0.27 ounces (2 ½ teaspoons) / 7.8 grams **instant yeast**, dry

0.35 ounces (1 ¾ teaspoons) / 10 grams **sea salt**

1/8 teaspoon ground **turmeric**

1.05 ounces (¼ cup) / 30 grams roasted **pumpkin seeds**, shelled, salted and more for topping

1 teaspoon **apple cider vinegar**

5.3 ounces (½ cup) / 150 grams **pumpkin puree**

0.95 ounces (2 tablespoons) / 27 grams **olive oil** and more for brushing

10.15 fluid ounce (1 ¼ cups) / 300 grams (300 ml) **water**, at 80°F / 25°C

Directions:

1.   Switch on the oven, then set it to 450°F / 230°C and let it preheat.

2.   Meanwhile, take a large mixing bowl, add vinegar, yeast, and pumpkin puree in it, pour in water and whisk until combined.

3.   Take a medium mixing bowl, place flour in it, stir in salt, sugar, and all the spices until combined, stir in oil and then fold in pumpkin seeds until evenly incorporated.

4.   Take a large baking sheet, line it with a parchment paper and place dough on it.

5. Shape the dough into a ball using lightly floured hands.

6. Brush oil on the surface of the loaf, make a ¼-inch / ½-cm deep X or slash on top of the dough by using a serrated knife and then sprinkle some more pumpkin seeds on top of the surface.

7. Place the baking sheet in a warm place and let the dough rest for 45 minutes until risen.

8. Then bake the bread for 50 minutes until the crust of bread turns nicely brown.

9. When done, transfer the bread to a wire rack, cool it for 30 minutes, then cut it into slices and serve.

(Don't cut the bread until it has cooled completely. The bread continues to bake even after it has been removed from the oven. Cutting too early may result in the inside becoming rubbery)

Chocolate Chunk Bread

Preparation time: 12 hours and 45 minutes

Cooking time: 45 minutes

Total time: 13 hours and 30 minutes

Servings: 1 loaf, about 12 slices

Nutritional Info (Per Serving):

120 Cal | 2 g Fat | 2 g Protein | 24 g Carbs | 1 g Fiber

Ingredients:

8.8 ounces (2 cups) / 250 grams **all-purpose flour**

4.25 ounces (1 cup) / 120 grams **whole-wheat flour**

0.05 ounces (½ teaspoon) / 1.5 grams **active yeast, dry**

0.3 ounces (1 ½ teaspoons) / 8.5 grams **sea salt**

1.45 ounces (3 tablespoons) / 40 grams **brown sugar**

2.65 ounces (½ cup) / 75 grams of **cocoa powder**

3.2 ounces (½ cup) / 90 grams **dark chocolate chips**

12 fluid ounces (1 ½ cup) / 355 grams (355 ml) **water**, at room temperature

Directions:

1. Prepare the dough and for this, take a large mixing bowl (preferably) with a resealable lid and then add flour in it along with salt, yeast, and sugar, stir until mixed.

2. Add chocolate chips, pour in water, mix by using a wooden spoon or a stand mixer until incorporated and sticky mixture comes together, and then fold in cocoa powder until just mixed.

3. Cover the bowl with its lid (or plastic wrap / aluminum foil) and then let the dough rest for a minimum of 12 hours at the room temperature until double in volume.

4. Meanwhile, spread the parchment sheet on a clean working sheet and then sprinkle some flour on top of it.

5. When the dough has risen, sprinkle some flour on the surface of the dough, pull up the dough, and then place it onto the prepared parchment sheet.

6.   Shape the dough into a ball and for this, lift its edges towards the center by using lightly floured hands, tuck in the edges to make it round, turn the dough around seam side down, and then pat the sides to make the dough more round.

7.   Place the dough ball with the parchment into a large bowl or a proofing basket and then let it rest for 30 minutes.

8.   During the resting time, switch on the oven, place a large pot or a Dutch oven with its lid into it, then set it to 425°F / 220°C and let it preheat.

9.   After the 30 minutes, sprinkle some more flour onto the dough, make a ¼-inch / ½-cm deep X or slash on top of the dough by using a serrated knife, and then carefully place it into the pot with the parchment paper.

10. Cover the pot with the lid, bake the bread for 30 minutes, then uncover the pot and continue baking for 15 minutes until the crust of bread turns nicely brown.

11. When done, transfer the bread to a wire rack, cool it for 30 minutes, then cut it into slices and serve.

(Don't cut the bread until it has cooled completely. The bread continues to bake even after it has been removed from the oven. Cutting too early may result in the inside becoming rubbery)

Spelt Loaf

Preparation time: 14 hours and 15 minutes

Cooking time: 45 minutes

Total time: 15 hours

Servings: 1 loaf, about 12 slices

Nutritional Info (Per Serving):

97 Cal | 4.6 g Fat | 2.4 g Protein | 13 g Carbs | 1.7 g Fiber

Ingredients:

21.15 ounces (5 cups) / 600 grams **spelt flour**

0.08 ounces (¾ teaspoon) / 2.3 grams **instant yeast**, dry

0.15 ounces (¾ teaspoon) / 4.3 grams **salt**

12 fluid ounces (1 ½ cups) / 355 grams (355 ml) **water**, at 80°F / 25°C

Directions:

1.   Prepare the dough and for this, take a large mixing bowl (preferably) with a resealable lid and then add all the ingredients except for water.

2.   Stir until mixed, pour in water, and then mix by using a wooden spoon or a stand mixer until incorporated and sticky mixture comes together.

3.   Cover the bowl with its lid (or plastic wrap / aluminum foil) and then let the dough rest for at least 14 hours at the room temperature until double in volume.

4.   Meanwhile, spread the parchment sheet on a clean working sheet and then sprinkle some flour on top of it.

5.   When the dough has risen, sprinkle some flour on the surface of the dough, pull up the dough, and then place it onto the prepared parchment sheet.

6.   Shape the dough into a ball and for this, lift its edges towards the center by using lightly floured hands, tuck in the edges to make it round, turn the dough around seam side down, and then pat the sides to make the dough more round.

7.   During the resting time, switch on the oven, place a large pot or a Dutch oven with its lid into it, then set it to 425°F / 220°C and let it preheat.

8.   Then carefully place it into the pot with the parchment paper, cover the pot with the lid, bake the bread for 30 minutes, then uncover the pot and continue baking for 15 minutes until the crust of bread turns nicely brown.

9.   When done, transfer the bread to a wire rack, cool it for 30 minutes, then cut it into slices and serve.

(Don't cut the bread until it has cooled completely. The bread continues to bake even after it has been removed from the oven. Cutting too early may result in the inside becoming rubbery)

Garlic and Parmesan Bread

Preparation time: 2 hour and 20 minutes

Cooking time: 20 minutes

Total time: 2 hour and 40 minutes

Servings: 1 loaf, about 12 slices

Nutritional Info (Per Serving):

232 Cal | 7.2 g Fat | 7 g Protein | 35 g Carbs | 2 g Fiber

Ingredients:

5.3 ounces / 150 grams **all-purpose flour**

0.16 ounces (½ tablespoon) / 4.7 grams **instant yeast**, dry

3 cloves minced **garlic**

1 teaspoon dried **rosemary**

0.1 ounces (½ teaspoon) / 2.8 grams **salt**

½ teaspoon dried **oregano**

0.22 ounces (½ tablespoon) / 6.25 grams **sugar**

½ teaspoon dried **basil**

0.25 ounces (½ tablespoon) / 7 grams **butter**, unsalted

0.5 ounces (1 tablespoon) / 13 grams **olive oil**

1.55 ounces (3 tablespoons) / 45 grams grated **parmesan cheese**

4 fluid ounces (½ cup) / 120 grams (120 ml) **water**, at 100°F / 38°C

Directions:

1.   Prepare the dough and for this, take a large mixing bowl (preferably) with a resealable lid, pour in water, stir in yeast and sugar until sugar has dissolved, and let it rest for 5 minutes.

2.   Then add salt, garlic, add the herbs and cheese and then gradually mix in flour by using a wooden spoon or a stand mixer until incorporated and sticky mixture comes together.

3. Cover the bowl with its lid (or plastic wrap / aluminum foil) and then let the dough rest for 2 hours at a warm place until double in volume.

4. Meanwhile, switch on the oven, then set it to 375°F / 190°C and let it preheat.

5. Take a baking sheet and then grease it with oil.

6. When the dough has risen, sprinkle some flour on the surface of the dough, pull up the dough, and then place it onto the prepared baking sheet.

7. Shape the dough into a ball using lightly floured hands.

8. Place the baking sheet into a warm place and let the dough rest for a minimum of 30 minutes until risen.

9. Then make a ¼-inch / ½-cm deep X or slash on top of the dough by using a serrated knife, spread butter on top, and bake it for 20 minutes until the crust of bread turns nicely brown.

10. When done, transfer the bread to a wire rack, cool it for 30 minutes, then cut it into slices and serve.

(Don't cut the bread until it has cooled completely. The bread continues to bake even after it has been removed from the oven. Cutting too early may result in the inside becoming rubbery)

French Bread Baguette

Preparation time: 6 hours and 5 minutes

Cooking time: 40 minutes

Total time: 6 hours and 45 minutes

Serving: 2 loaves

Nutritional Info (Per Serving):

220 Cal | 2 g Fat | 8.7 g Protein | 42 g Carb | 1.7 g Fiber

Ingredients:

10.6 ounces (2.4 cups) / 300 grams **all-purpose flour**

0.14 ounces (1 teaspoon) / 4 grams **sugar**

0.3 ounces (3 teaspoons) / 9 grams **active yeast**, dry

0.2 ounces (1 teaspoon) / 5.7 grams **salt**

7.45 fluid ounces (1 cup) / 220 grams (220 ml) **water**, at 80°F / 25°C

Directions:

1.   Prepare the dough and for this, take a small mixing bowl (preferably) with a resealable lid, pour in 2 tablespoons of water, stir in yeast and sugar until sugar has dissolved, and let it rest for 5 minutes.

2.   Then take a large bowl, place flour in it, add salt and yeast mixture, pour in the remaining water, and then gradually mix it using a wooden spoon or a stand mixer until incorporated and sticky mixture comes together.

3.   Cover the bowl with its lid (or plastic wrap / aluminum foil) and then let the dough rest for a minimum of 10 hours in the refrigerator until doubled in volume.

4.   Meanwhile, spread the parchment sheet on a clean working sheet and then sprinkle some flour on top of it.

5.   When the dough has risen, sprinkle some flour on the surface of the dough, pull up the dough, and then place it onto the prepared parchment sheet.

6.   Gently press and shape the dough into a rectangle, then gently fold its sides towards the middle like an envelope, cover it with a cling film and let it rest at a warm place for 45 minutes.

7.   After the 45 minutes, shape the dough into a rectangle again and fold the sides in the same manner, cover it with a cling film, and continue it rest for another 45 minutes.

8.   Then transfer the dough to a clean working space dusted with flour and divide it into two parts.

9.   Shape each part of the dough into a 13-inch / 33-cm log, and for this, flatten the dough out slightly, then fold the sides into the middle and shape into a log.

10.   Then take a baguette baking tray, dust it with flour, place prepared dough logs on the tray and let them rest at a warm place for 45 minutes.

11.   Meanwhile, switch on the oven, place a tray or heatproof bowl filled with water in its bottom, then set it to 425°F / 220°C and let it preheat.

12.   After the 45 minutes, dust dough logs with flour, then make four ¼-inch / ½-cm deep slashes on top of both baguettes by using a serrated knife and bake them for approximately 40 minutes until the crust of bread turns nicely brown.

13.   When done, transfer the baguettes to the wire rack, cool them for 30 minutes, then   cut   into   slices   and   serve.

Kneaded Artisan Bread Recipes

Simple Kneaded Artisan Bread

Preparation time: 2 hours and 50 minutes

Cooking time: 45 minutes

Total time: 3 hours and 35 minutes

Servings: 1 loaf, about 12 slices

Nutritional Info (Per Serving):

261.7 Cal | 1 g Fat | 8.5 g Protein | 55.8 g Carbs | 4 g Fiber

Ingredients:

8.8 ounces (2 cups) / 250 grams **all-purpose flour**

8.45 ounces (2 cups) / 240 grams **whole-wheat flour**

0.11 ounces (1 teaspoon) / 3 grams **active yeast**, dry

0.2 ounces (1 teaspoon) / 5.7 grams **salt**

12 fluid ounces (1 ½ cups) / 355 grams (355 ml) **water**, at 100°F / 38°C

Directions:

1.   Prepare the dough and for this, take a large mixing bowl (preferably) with a resealable lid and then add flour in it along with salt and yeast.

2.   Stir until mixed, pour in water, and then mix by using a wooden spoon or a stand mixer until incorporated and sticky mixture comes together.

3.   Cover the bowl with its lid (or plastic wrap / aluminum foil) and then let the dough rest for a minimum of 2 hours or more at a warm place until double in volume.

4.   Meanwhile, spread the parchment sheet on a clean working sheet and then sprinkle some flour on top of it.

5.   When the dough has risen, sprinkle some flour on the surface of the dough, pull up the dough, and then place it onto the prepared parchment sheet.

6.   Knead the dough for 5 minutes or more to remove air bubbles from it and then shape it into a ball.

7.   For this, lift its edges towards the center by using lightly floured hands, tuck in the edges to make it round, turn the dough around seam side down, and then pat the sides to make the dough more round.

8.   Place the dough ball with the parchment into a Dutch oven or a large pot, cover with the lid and then let it rest for 30 minutes.

9.   During the resting time, switch on the oven, then set it to 450°F / 230°C and let it preheat.

10. After the 30 minutes, sprinkle some more flour onto the dough, make a ¼-inch / ½-cm deep X or slash on top of the dough by using a serrated knife, and then carefully place the pot into the oven.

11. Cover the pot with the lid, bake the bread for 30 minutes, uncover the pot, switch the temperature to 375°F / 190°C and then continue baking for 15 minutes until the crust of bread turns nicely brown.

12. When done, transfer the bread to a wire rack, cool it for 30 minutes, then cut it into slices and serve.

(Don't cut the bread until it has cooled completely. The bread continues to bake even after it has been removed from the oven. Cutting too early may result in the inside becoming rubbery)

Savory Bread

Preparation time: 27 hours and 40 minutes

Cooking time: 45 minutes

Total time: 28 hours and 25 minutes

Servings: 1 loaf, about 12 slices

Nutritional Info (Per Serving):

117.5 Cal | 2.3 g Fat | 4.6 g Protein | 21.7 g Carbs | 4.2 g Fiber

Ingredients:

For The Sponge:

2.65 ounces (½ cup + 1 tablespoon) / 75 grams **all-purpose flour**

2.65 ounces (½ cup + 2 tablespoons) / 75 grams **whole-wheat flour**

0.06 ounces (¼ teaspoon) / 0.8 grams **active yeast**, dry

5.25 fluid ounces (2/3 cup) / 160 grams (160 ml) **water**, at 80°F / 25°C

For The Final Dough:

5 ounces (1 cup + 2 tablespoons) / 140 grams **all-purpose flour**

2.65 ounces (½ cup + 2 tablespoons) / 75 grams **whole-wheat flour**

0.15 ounces (¾ teaspoon) / 4.3 grams **sea salt**

0.5 ounces (1 tablespoon) / 13 grams **olive oil**

3.65 fluid ounces (½ cup) / 120 grams (120 ml) **water**, at 80°F / 25°C

Directions:

1.   Prepare the sponge, and for this, take a medium bowl (preferably) with a resealable lid, and then add all-purpose flour and whole-wheat flour along with yeast and water.

2.   Mix the ingredients until well combined, cover the bowl with its lid (or plastic wrap / aluminum foil), and then let the dough rest for a minimum of 24 hours at the room temperature until double in volume.

3. Then take a large mixing bowl (preferably) with a resealable lid, add remaining ingredients in it along with the risen sponge.

4. Knead all the ingredients until incorporated and sticky mixture comes together, cover the bowl with its lid (or plastic wrap / aluminum foil), and then let the dough rest for 1 hour or more at a warm place until risen.

5. Meanwhile, spread the parchment sheet on a clean working sheet and then sprinkle some flour on top of it.

6. When the dough has risen, sprinkle some flour on the surface of the dough, pull up the dough, and then place it onto the prepared parchment sheet.

7. Knead the dough for 5 minutes or more to remove air bubbles from it and then shape it into a ball.

8. For this, lift its edges towards the center by using lightly floured hands, tuck in the edges to make it round, turn the dough around seam side down, and then pat the sides to make the dough more round.

9. Place the dough ball with the parchment into a large bowl or a proofing basket and then let it rest for 2 hours.

10. During the resting time, switch on the oven, place a large pot or a Dutch oven with its lid into it, then set it to 450°F / 230°C and let it preheat.

11. After the 2 hours, sprinkle some more flour onto the dough, make a ¼-inch / ½-cm deep X or slash on top of the dough by using a serrated knife, and then carefully place it into the pot with the parchment paper.

12. Cover the pot with the lid, bake the bread for 30 minutes, then uncover the pot and continue baking for 15 minutes until the crust of bread turns nicely brown.

13. When done, transfer the bread to a wire rack, cool it for 30 minutes, then cut it into slices and serve.

Tuscan Herb Bread

Preparation time: 4 hours and 20 minutes

Cooking time: 45 minutes

Total time: 5 hours and 5 minutes

Servings: 1 loaf, about 12 slices

Nutritional Info (Per Serving):

123 Cal | 1 g Fat | 5 g Protein | 22 g Carbs | 4 g Fiber

Ingredients:

13.4 ounces (3 cups) / 380 grams **bread flour**

½ teaspoon dried **thyme**

0.16 ounces (1 ½ teaspoons) / 4.7 grams **instant yeast**, dry

½ teaspoon dried **oregano**

0.3 ounces (1 ½ teaspoons) / 8.5 grams **salt**

½ teaspoon dried **basil**

0.22 ounces (1 ½ teaspoons) / 6.25 grams **sugar**

½ teaspoon dried **marjoram**

0.7 ounces (1 ½ tablespoons) / 20 grams **olive oil**

12 fluid ounces (1 ½ cups) / 355 grams (355 ml) **water**, at 80°F / 25°C

Directions:

1.   Take a large mixing bowl (preferably) with a resealable lid and then add flour in it along with salt, yeast, sugar, and all the herbs.

2.   Stir until mixed, add olive oil, pour in water, and then mix by using a wooden spoon or a stand mixer until incorporated and sticky mixture comes together.

3.   Cover the bowl with its lid (or plastic wrap / aluminum foil) and then let the dough rest for a minimum of 2 hours at a warm place until double in volume.

4.   Meanwhile, spread the parchment sheet on a clean working sheet and then sprinkle some flour on top of it.

5.   When the dough has risen, sprinkle some flour on the surface of the dough, pull up the dough, and then place it onto the prepared parchment sheet.

6.   Knead the dough for 5 minutes or more to remove air bubbles from it and then shape it into a ball.

7.   For this, lift its edges towards the center by using lightly floured hands, tuck in the edges to make it round, turn the dough around seam side down, and then pat the sides to make the dough more round.

8.   Place the dough ball with the parchment into a Dutch oven or a large pot, cover with the lid and then let it rest for at least 2 hours.

9.   During the resting time, switch on the oven, then set it to 450°F / 230°C and let it preheat.

10. After the 2 hours, sprinkle some more flour onto the dough, make a ¼-inch / ½-cm deep X or slash on top of the dough by using a serrated knife, and cover the pot with the lid.

11. Carefully place the pot into the oven, bake the bread for 30 minutes, uncover the pot, switch the temperature to 375°F / 190°C and then continue baking for 15 minutes until the crust of bread turns nicely brown.

12. When done, transfer the bread to a wire rack, cool it for 30 minutes, then cut it into slices and serve.

(Don't cut the bread until it has cooled completely. The bread continues to bake even after it has been removed from the oven. Cutting too early may result in the inside becoming rubbery)

Einkorn Bread

Preparation time: 23 hours and 30 minutes

Cooking time: 45 minutes

Total time: 24 hours and 15 minutes

Servings: 1 loaf, about 12 slices

Nutritional Info (Per Serving):

102 Cal | 1 g Fat | 4 g Protein | 20 g Carbs | 2 g Fiber

Ingredients:

For The Sponge:

6.7 ounces (1 2/3 cups) / 190 grams **einkorn flour**

0.02 ounces (1/8 teaspoon) / 0.4 grams **instant yeast**, dry

4.75 fluid ounces (2/3 cup) / 140 grams (140 ml) **water**, at 55°F / 25°C

For The Final Dough:

7.4 ounces (1 ¾ cups) / 210 grams **einkorn flour**

0.05 ounces (½ teaspoon) / 1.5 grams **instant yeast**

0.40 ounces (2 teaspoons) / 11 grams **salt**

4.75 fluid ounces (2/3 cup) / 140 grams (140 ml) **water**, at 70°F / 20°C

Directions:

1.   Prepare the sponge, and for this, take a medium bowl (preferably) with a resealable lid, add flour along with yeast, and then pour in the water, mix the ingredients until well combined.

2.   Cover the bowl with its lid (or plastic wrap / aluminum foil) and then let the sponge rest for a minimum of 20 hours at the room temperature until double in volume.

3.   Then take a large mixing bowl (preferably) with a resealable lid, add remaining ingredients in it along with the risen sponge.

4. Knead all the ingredients until incorporated and sticky mixture comes together, cover the bowl with its lid (or plastic wrap / aluminum foil), and then let the dough rest for 1 hour or more at a warm place until risen.

5. Meanwhile, spread the parchment sheet on a clean working sheet and then sprinkle some flour on top of it.

6. When the dough has risen, sprinkle some flour on the surface of the dough, pull up the dough, and then place it onto the prepared parchment sheet.

7. Knead the dough for 5 minutes or more to remove air bubbles from it, and then shape it into a ball.

8. For this, lift its edges towards the center by using lightly floured hands, tuck in the edges to make it round, turn the dough around seam side down, and then pat the sides to make the dough more round.

9. Place the dough ball with the parchment into a large bowl or a proofing basket and then let it rest for 2 hours at a warm place.

10. During the resting time, switch on the oven, place a large pot or a Dutch oven with its lid into it, then set it to 500°F / 260°C and let it preheat.

11. After the 2 hours, sprinkle some more flour onto the dough, make a ¼-inch / ½-cm deep X or slash on top of the dough by using a serrated knife, and then carefully place it into the pot with the parchment paper.

12. Cover the pot with the lid, bake the bread for 30 minutes, uncover the pot, switch the temperature to 425°F / 220°C and then continue baking for 15 minutes until the crust of bread turns nicely brown.

13. When done, transfer the bread to a wire rack, cool it for 30 minutes, then cut it into slices and serve.

(Don't cut the bread until it has cooled completely. The bread continues to bake even after it has been removed from the oven. Cutting too early may result in the inside becoming rubbery)

Tomato, Basil and Garlic Bread

Preparation time: 4 hours and 45 minutes

Cooking time: 45 minutes

Total time: 4 hours and 30 minutes

Servings: 1 loaf, about 6 slices

Nutritional Info (Per Serving):

275 Cal | 3.1 g Fat | 8 g Protein | 53.4 g Carbs | 3 g Fiber

Ingredients:

1 ounce (½ cup) / 25 grams chopped **sun-dried tomatoes**

13.2 ounces (3 cups) / 375 grams **all-purpose flour**

0.25 ounces (2 ¼ teaspoons) / 7 grams **active yeast**, dry

1 teaspoon **minced garlic**

0.3 ounces (1 ½ teaspoons) / 8.5 grams **salt**

1 tablespoon **dried basil**

0.14 ounces (1 teaspoon) / 4 grams **sugar**

0.5 ounces (1 tablespoon) / 13 grams **olive oil**

10.15 fluid ounces (1 ¼ cups) / 300 grams (300 ml) **water**, at 100°F / 38°C

Directions:

1. Take a large mixing bowl (preferably) with a resealable lid and then add 8.8 ounces (2 cups) / 250 grams flour in it along with salt, yeast, and sugar.

2. Stir until mixed, add olive oil, pour in water, mix by using a wooden spoon or a stand mixer until incorporated, and then mix in remaining flour until dough comes together.

3. Cover the bowl with its lid (or plastic wrap / aluminum foil) and then let the dough rest for a minimum of 4 hours in the refrigerator until doubled in volume.

4. Meanwhile, spread the parchment sheet on a clean working sheet and then sprinkle some flour on top of it.

5. When the dough has risen, add remaining ingredients in it and then knead until well mixed.

6.   Shape the dough into a ball and for this, lift its edges towards the center by using lightly floured hands, tuck in the edges to make it round, turn the dough around seam side down, and then pat the sides to make the dough more round.

7.   Place the dough ball with the parchment into a Dutch oven or a large pot, cover with the lid and then let it rest for 30 minutes at a warm place.

8.   During the resting time, switch on the oven, set it to 350°F / 175°C and let it preheat.

9.   After the 30 minutes, sprinkle some more flour onto the dough, make a ¼-inch / ½-cm deep X or slash on top of the dough by using a serrated knife, and then carefully place the pot into the oven.

10. Cover the pot with the lid, bake the bread for 30 minutes, uncover the pot, and then continue baking for 15 minutes until the crust of bread turns nicely brown.

11. When done, transfer the bread to a wire rack, cool it for 30 minutes, then cut it into slices and serve.

(Don't cut the bread until it has cooled completely. The bread continues to bake even after it has been removed from the oven. Cutting too early may result in the inside becoming rubbery)

Gluten-Free Bread

Preparation time: 1 hour and 30 minutes

Cooking time: 45 minutes

Total time: 2 hours and 15 minutes

Servings: 1 loaf, about 12 slices

Nutritional Info (Per Serving):

83 Cal | 2.2 g Fat | 1.5 g Protein | 14 g Carbs | 1.5 g Fiber

Ingredients:

1.95 ounces (0.45 cup) / 55 grams **tapioca flour**

8.1 ounces (1 ¾ cups + 1 tablespoon) / 230 grams of **gluten-free flour**

0.22 ounces (2 teaspoons) / 6.2 grams **instant yeast**, dry

0.33 ounces (1 ¼ teaspoons) / 9.2 grams **xanthan gum**

0.04 ounces (¼ teaspoon) / 1.2 grams **baking soda**

0.28 ounces (2 teaspoons) / 8 grams **sugar**

0.2 ounces (1 teaspoon) / 5.7 grams **salt**

0.5 ounces (1 tablespoon) / 13 grams **olive oil**

1 **egg**, at room temperature

8 fluid ounces (1 cup) / 250 grams (240 ml) **milk**, at 95°F / 35°C

Directions:

1.   Prepare the dough and for this, take a large mixing bowl (preferably) with a resealable lid and then add both flours in it along with yeast, sugar, salt, xanthan gum, and baking soda, mix until well combined.

2.   Make a well in the center of the bowl, add egg and oil, pour in the milk, and then knead until incorporated and the dough comes together.

3.   Take a Dutch oven or a large pot, grease it with oil, place dough in it, cover with its lid, and then place it in a warm place for 75 minutes until doubled in size.

4.   During the resting time, switch on the oven, set it to 375°F / 190°C and let it preheat.

5.   When the dough has risen, sprinkle some more flour on its surface, and then make a ¼-inch / ½-cm deep X or slash on top by using a serrated knife.

6.   Place the pot into the oven and bake the bread for 30 minutes until the crust of bread turns nicely brown.

7.   Remove pot from the oven, turn the loaf so that it is up-side-down and continue baking for 15 minutes until the crust of bread turns brown on all sides.

8.   When done, transfer the bread to a wire rack, cool it for 30 minutes, then cut it into slices and serve.

(Don't cut the bread until it has cooled completely. The bread continues to bake even after it has been removed from the oven. Cutting too early may result in the inside becoming rubbery)

Thanks for buying *Artisan Bread Recipes!*

If you found the recipes amazing and delicious, please share your thoughts, successes and failures on the amazon sales page of this book.

About The Author

Marie Folher grew up in Strasbourg, France and she fell in love with baking as a kid. She moved to California at the age of 21 and she found a job from a small bakery. Since then, she has baked countless amount of different baked goods. She's had time to experiment countless different flavour combinations, and with trial and error she has found, and still finds, amazing recipes. With her cookbooks, she wants to share her best recipes with you.

Other Books by Marie Folher

Bundt Cake Recipes – 30 Delicious Bundt Cake Recipes From Scratch

Keto Chaffle Recipes – 30 Easy Fast and Super Delicious Ketogenic Chaffle Recipes

Keto Bread Machine Recipes –30 Easy, Healthy and Low-Carb Ketogenic Bread Machine Recipes

Keto Bread Recipes – 30 Easy, Healthy and Super Delicious Low-Carb Ketogenic Bread Recipes

Bread Machine Cookbook – Simple and Easy-To-Follow Bread Machine Recipes for Mouthwatering Homemade Bread

Image Credits

Cover image: Designed by azerbaijan_stockers / Freepik

Raisin Nut Bread: iStock.com/Lynne Mitchell

Whole Wheat Bread: iStock.com/vikif

Garlic and Rosemary Bread: iStock.com/Enzo Nguyen@Tercer Ojo Photography

Herb Crusted Artisan Bread: iStock.com/porosolka

Multigrain Bread: iStock.com/nevarpp

Sourdough Bread: iStock.com/Foxys_forest_manufacture

Cinnamon and Raisins Bread: iStock.com/phototropic

Garlic and Sesame Seed Bread: iStock.com/DebbiSmirnoff

Cranberries and Walnut Bread: iStock.com/Merrimon

Blueberries and Walnut Bread: iStock.com/DanielLacy

Cinnamon, Raisin and Pecan Bread: iStock.com/clubfoto

Jalapeno Cheese Bread: iStock.com/fotogal

Italian Bread: iStock.com/apomares

Basil and Onion Bread: iStock.com/letty17

Rosemary and Lemon Bread: iStock.com/anandaBGD

Olive Bread: iStock.com/sjenner13

Graham Bread: iStock.com/tonymax

Whole-Wheat Walnut Bread: iStock.com/DebbiSmirnoff

Lemon and Thyme Bread: iStock.com/nataliaspb

Pumpkin Spice Bread: iStock.com/bgwalker

Chocolate Chunk Bread: iStock.com/Enzo Nguyen@Tercer Ojo Photography

Spelt Loaf: iStock.com/muratkoc

Garlic and Parmesan Bread: iStock.com/modesigns58

French Bread Baguette: iStock.com/chictype

Simple Kneaded Artisan Bread: iStock.com/sjenner13

Savory Bread: iStock.com/Enzo Nguyen@Tercer Ojo Photography

Tuscan Herb Bread: iStock.com/Mizina

Einkorn Bread: iStock.com/gerenme

Tomato, Basil and Garlic Bread: iStock.com/photosimysia

Gluten-Free Bread: iStock.com/fcafotodigital

Printed in Great Britain
by Amazon